99 Ways to Tell a Story

Also by Matt Madden

BLACK CANDY
(Black Eye Books)

ODDS OFF
(Highwater Books)

99 Ways to Tell a Story: Exercises in Style

Matt Madden

Chamberlain Bros.
a member of Penguin Group (USA) Inc.
New York
2005

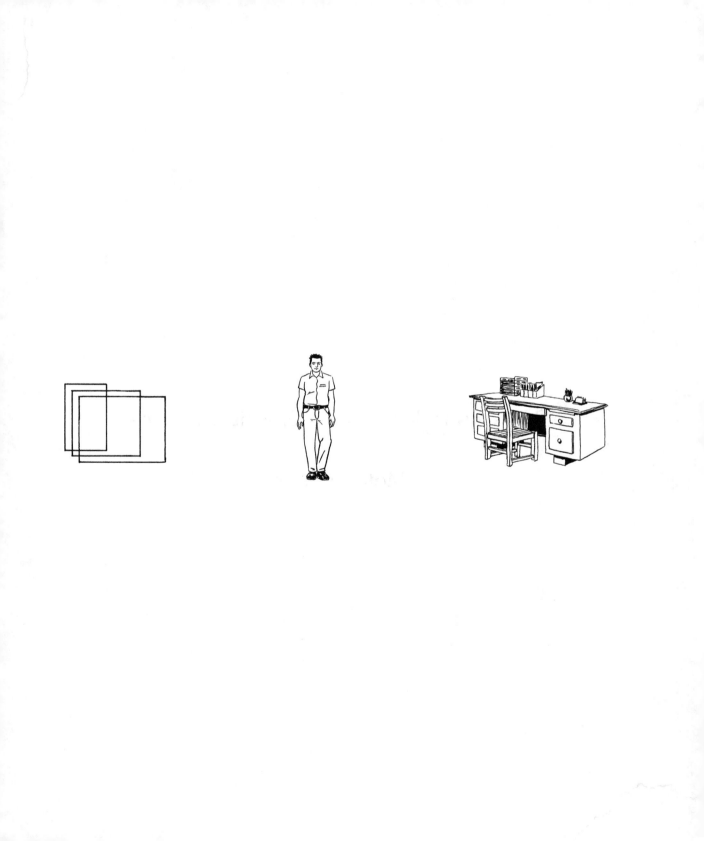

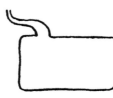

15

?!.:,.

aefg
hik
lmn
ors
twy

ITW

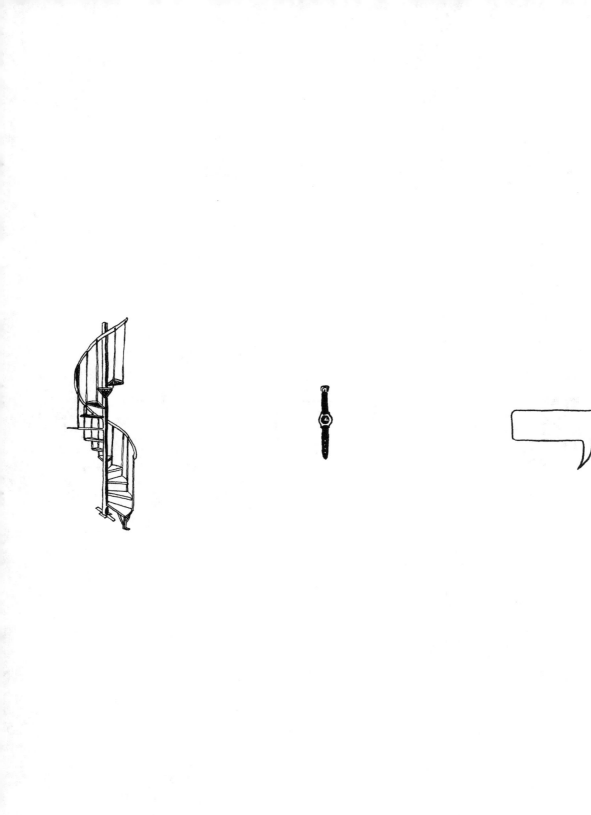

CHAMBERLAIN BROS.
Published by the Penguin Group
Penguin Group (USA) Inc., 375 Hudson Street, New York, New York 10014, USA
Penguin Group (Canada), 90 Eglinton Avenue East, Suite 700, Toronto, Ontario M4P 2Y3, Canada
(a division of Pearson Penguin Canada Inc.)
Penguin Books Ltd, 80 Strand, London WC2R 0RL, England
Penguin Ireland, 25 St Stephen's Green, Dublin 2, Ireland (a division of Penguin Books Ltd)
Penguin Group (Australia), 250 Camberwell Road, Camberwell, Victoria 3124, Australia
(a division of Pearson Australia Group Pty Ltd)
Penguin Books India Pvt Ltd, 11 Community Centre, Panchsheel Park, New Delhi—110 017, India
Penguin Group (NZ), Cnr Airborne and Rosedale Roads, Albany, Auckland 1310, New Zealand
(a division of Pearson New Zealand Ltd)
Penguin Books (South Africa) (Pty) Ltd, 24 Sturdee Avenue, Rosebank,
Johannesburg 2196, South Africa

Penguin Books Ltd, Registered Offices: 80 Strand, London WC2R 0RL, England

An application has been submitted to register this book with the Library of Congress.
ISBN 1-59609-078-2

Printed in the United States of America
5   7   9   10   8   6

This book is printed on acid-free paper. ∞

Book design by Charles Orr

The author would like to acknowledge his debt to Raymond Queneau, whose influence extends well beyond the inspiration for this book.

Contents

Introduction

Each comic in this book presents the same story—recounts exactly the same events—but takes a different approach to telling the tale. You will find varying points of view, different styles of drawing, homages and parodies, as well as interpretations that may challenge your idea of what exactly narrative is. For example, can a map tell a story? How about a page full of advertisements? I'm not suggesting that there's a definite answer, only that it's exciting to consider how many ways a story can be told, how art and text interact, and how these comics relate to other visual and narrative media.

This book was inspired by Raymond Queneau's *Exercises in Style* in which he spun ninety-nine variations out of a basic, two-part text relating two chance encounters with a mildly irritating character during the course of a day. He started by telling it in every conceivable tense, then by doing it in free verse, and then as a sonnet, as a telegram, in pig latin, as a series of exclamations, in an indifferent voice . . . you name it, he did it.

From the first time I read *Exercises in Style*, I thought it would be fun and challenging to apply the idea to a visual narrative, but dismissed it as a crazy notion. However, years went by and still the concept kept coming back to nudge me toward the drawing table. Six years ago, I finally gave in and put pen to paper. The reaction among my peers, friends, and family to the first few exercises was instantaneous and enthusiastic: I knew I had no choice but to see this through to the end.

Although there is a certain sequence to these pages, it is perfectly allowable to read the exercises in random order. Nor is there any requirement to read every comic in one sitting (or ever). Your first dive into these pages will make you want to come back from time to time in order to browse through the book, look up a favorite comic, or show it to a friend, much as you would with a collection of poetry or drawings.

Can a story, however simple or mundane, be separated from the manner in which it is told? Is there an essential nugget from which all stylistic and physical characteristics can be stripped? What would that core look like? This book begins with a comic I named "Template" because it has the least overt manipulation of formal elements. Yet even a moment's consideration yields a series of questions: Why is it drawn in pen and not with a brush? Why is it told in eight panels and how were they chosen? The style is not "cartoony," yet it is not quite "realistic"—Why? Suddenly it's clear that what appear to be merely "stylistic" choices are in fact an essential part of the story. In reading these comics you have the opportunity to question the effects that ways of telling have on what is being told, and, just as important, to enjoy the rich variety of approaches available to the artist, in comics and in other media.

Rather than rehashing the eternal battle between form and content, style and substance, I hope this work questions those tired dichotomies and suggests a different model: form *as* content, and substance inseparable from style.

—Matt Madden

Template

Monologue

Subjective

Upstairs

A Refrigerator with a View

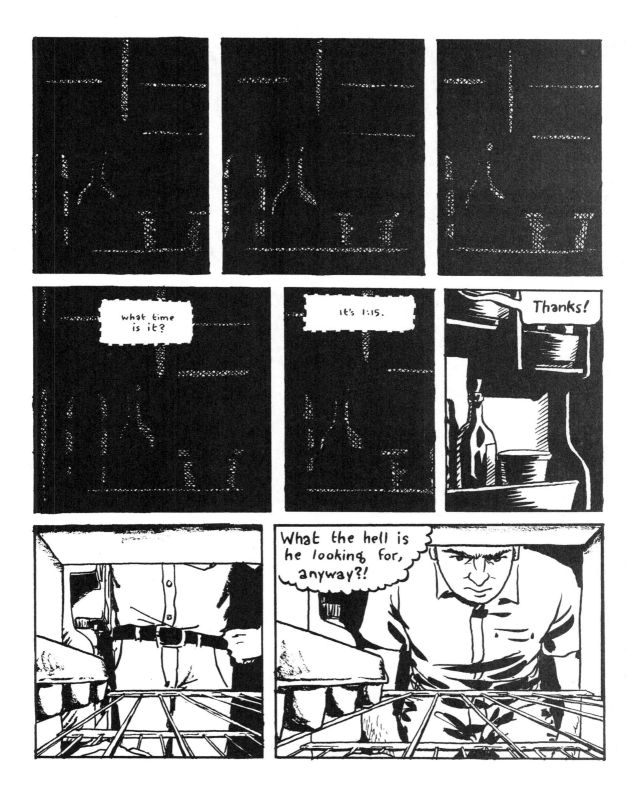

Voyeur

Sound Effects

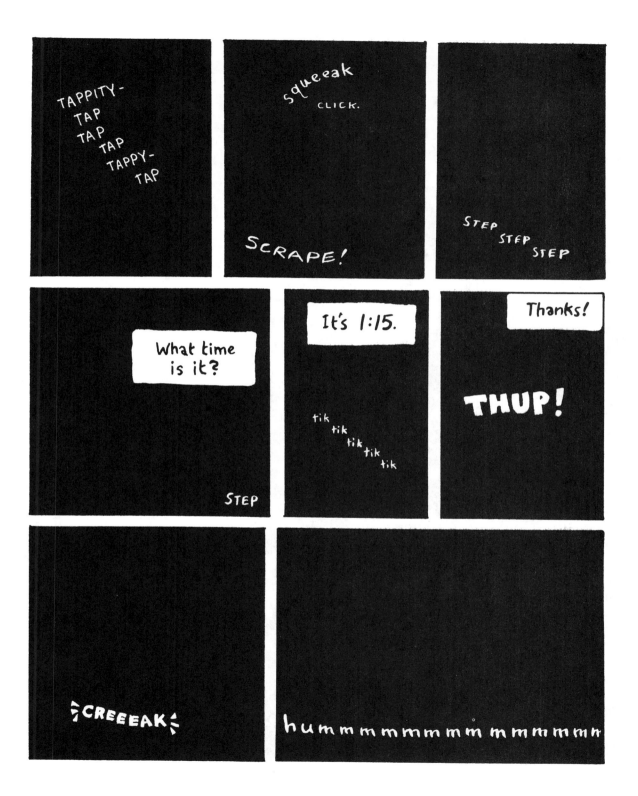

Emanata

Inventory

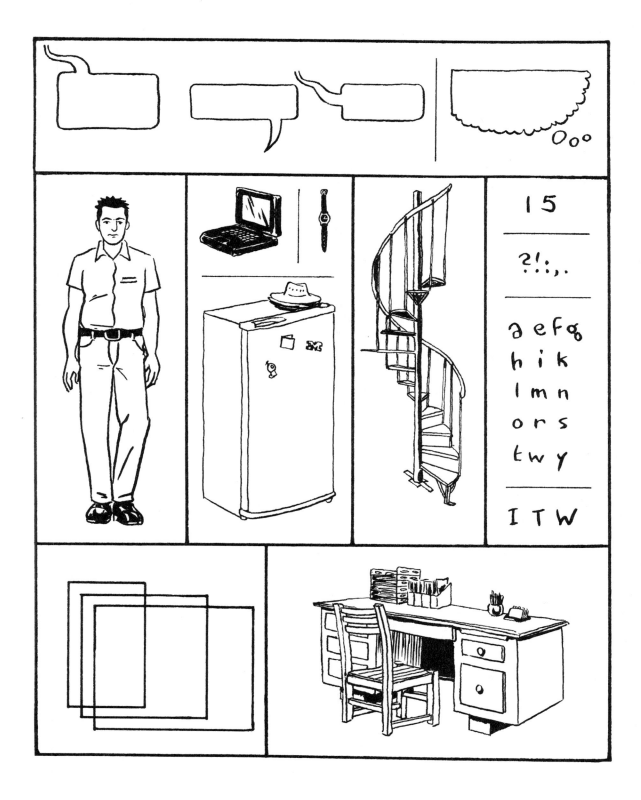

How-To

Welcome to
"Exercises in Style"

Retrograde

Tense

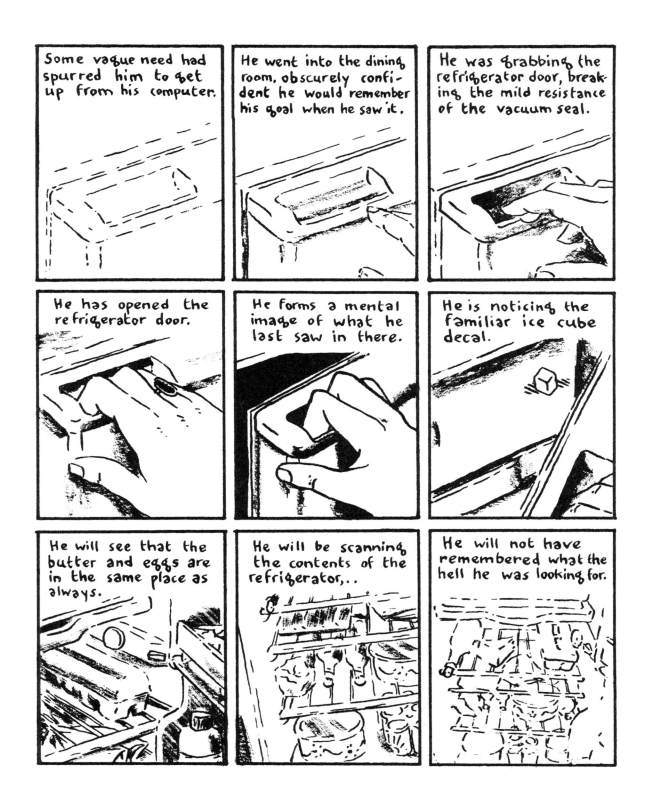

Flashback

Déjà Vu

Unreliable Narrator

Dailies

MacHinery, P.I.

By Clint Smith

Life with Biggsie

By Brube

Poopsie the Cat

By MUGS

Political Cartoon

Photocomic

Underground Comix

Manga

War Exercise

Exercises in Love

"YESTERDAY I ACCEPTED AN OFFER OF MARRIAGE FROM **BRADLEY BENTON**, BRANCH MANAGER FOR THE ENTIRE EASTERN DIVISION!

"I WAS THROUGH WITH THOSE WILD TYPES I USED TO DATE -- AND THE DAMAGE THEY DID TO MY REPUTATION...

"TONIGHT I WAS GOING TO MEET BRADLEY'S PARENTS -- MY FUTURE IN-LAWS!

"THEN SUDDENLY A HUSKY, MASCULINE VOICE PENETRATED MY INNOCENT BLISS...

WHAT TIME IS IT?

"I COULD FEEL MY HEART BEGINNING TO BEAT IN EXCITED, CONFUSED PALPITATIONS...

IT'S... 1:15.

"NO! I PROMISED MYSELF TO BRADLEY BENTON!

THANKS, DOLL!

"AND YET THE STRANGER'S THANKS PIERCED ME LIKE ARROWS LACED WITH SOME STRANGE ELIXIR!

OH, BRADLEY, I'M SORRY!

"WHAT THE HELL WAS I LOOKING FOR, ANYWAY?"

Fantasy

Plan 99 from Outer Space

High Noon

Police Procedural

Humor Comic

Furry

One Panel

Thirty Panels

Plus One

Etcetera

Opposites

Reframing
(Hands and Punctuation Marks)

Inking Outside the Box

Palindrome

Anagram I:
In Exercises, Style

Anagram II:
Le Teeny Sex Crisis

After Rodolphe Töppfer
(English Bootleg Version)

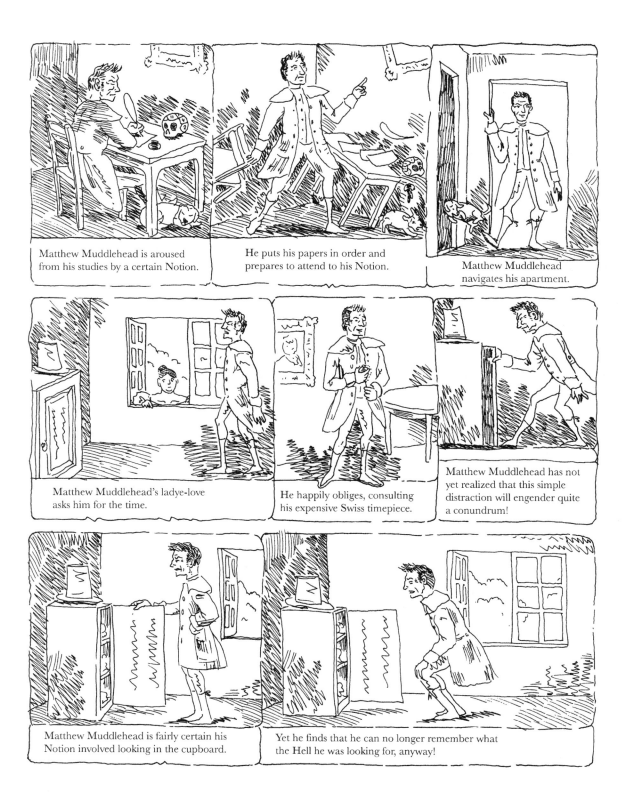

Matthew Muddlehead is aroused from his studies by a certain Notion.

He puts his papers in order and prepares to attend to his Notion.

Matthew Muddlehead navigates his apartment.

Matthew Muddlehead's ladye-love asks him for the time.

He happily obliges, consulting his expensive Swiss timepiece.

Matthew Muddlehead has not yet realized that this simple distraction will engender quite a conundrum!

Matthew Muddlehead is fairly certain his Notion involved looking in the cupboard.

Yet he finds that he can no longer remember what the Hell he was looking for, anyway!

A Newly Discovered Fragment
of the Bayeux Tapestry

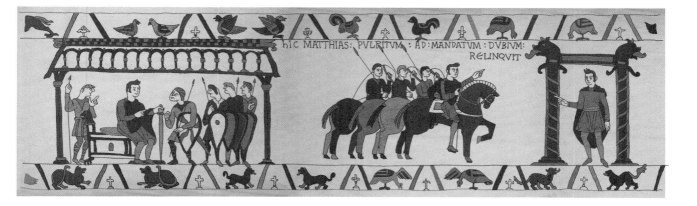

hIC MATTHIAS : PVLRITVM : AD : MANDATVM : DVBIVM : RELINQVIT

hIC IESSICA :

QVID : HORA : EST : INQVIT

ET hIC :

RESPONDIT : MATTHIAS

AD : GLACIE : CISTAM :

hIC MATTHIAS : IPSE : ROGAT : QVICQVID : QVAEREBAT

What Happens When the Ice
Truck Comes to Hogan's Alley
(after Richard F. Outcault)

Exorcise in Style

Dynamic Constraint

Ligne Claire

Superhero

Map

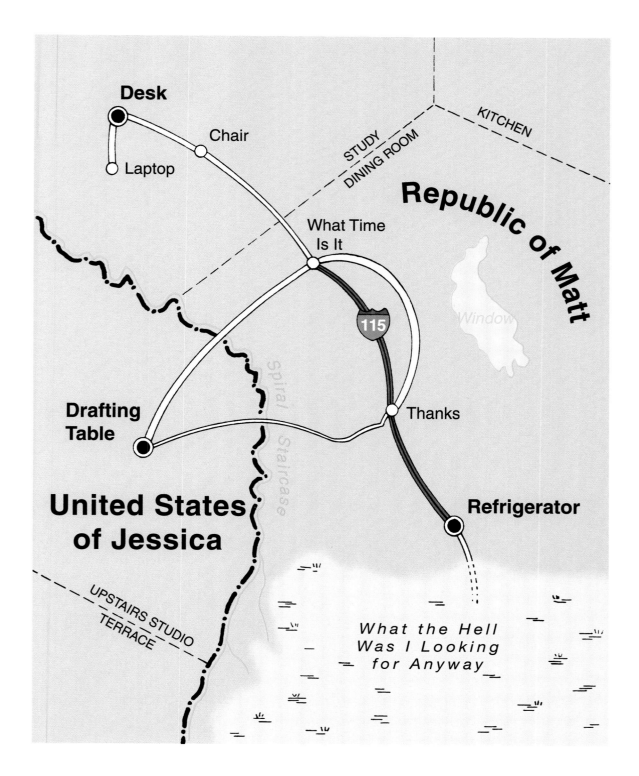

ROYGBIV

Exercises of a Rarebit Fiend
(after Winsor McCay)

Esk Her Size end Style
(after George Herriman)

Homage to Jack Kirby

Exercises in Closure
(after Scott McCloud)

1. MOMENT-TO-MOMENT

2. ACTION-TO-ACTION

3. SUBJECT-TO-SUBJECT

4. SCENE-TO-SCENE

5. ASPECT-TO-ASPECT

6. NON-SEQUITUR

Public Service Announcement

Paranoid Religious Tract

Cento
(David Mazzucchelli, Ben Katchor,
Chester Brown, Marc-Antoine Mathieu,
Daniel Clowes, Art Spiegelman,
Julie Doucet, Gary Panter)

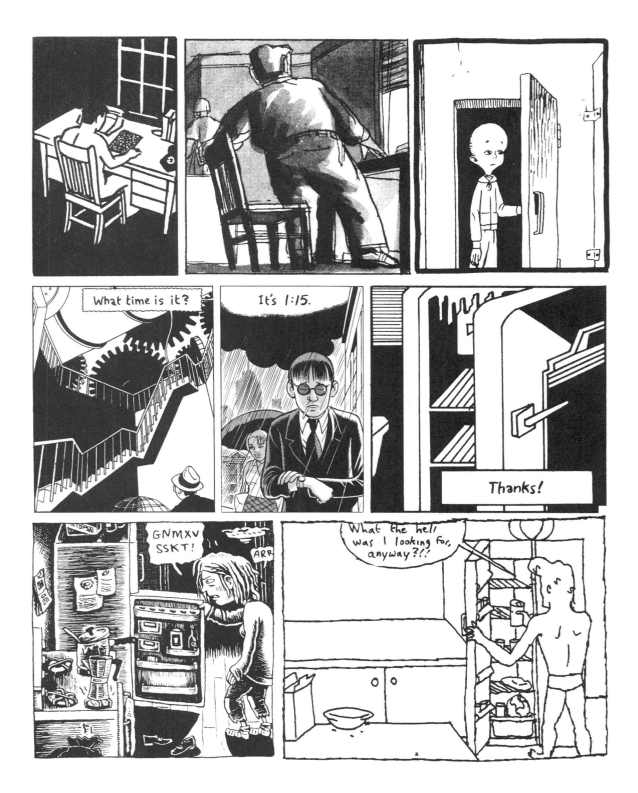

Two-in-One (Madden/Queneau)

Digital

0011011000011011001101010011011001110011010101010101110011011100101011001 1
0010101110011011100101011100110100110110011011001101011100110101010110011 0
1011100110110101111001101011100110101111001100110110011001010011011001110
0110101010101011001101110010101110011010011011001100011011001100100110001 1
0110011001010111001101011100110101010101110011010110011011010101110011011 1 0
0110101010111001101011100110110101110011010101011100110101111011100110101 0 1
0111001101011001101101001010101010110011010111100111110011011100101011100
1100110100110110010100111110011010101011100110101110011010011011001010011 0 1
1001100110101010101011100110111001010111001100110100110110010100110110011 1
0011010111001101010101110011010111001101101011110011010111001101010101110 0
1101011100110110101110011010110011010101011100110101110011010011011001010 0 1
1011100110101111100000011011001110011010101010101011100110111001010111001 1 0
1010101011100101010101011100110111001010110011001101001101100101001101101 1 1
0010111001100110100110110010100111110011010101011001101011010111001101010 1
1100110101110011011010111001101011111100110101110011010101011100110101110 1 1
0110101110111001101010101110011010111001101101010111100110101110011010010 0 1 0 1 0
0101011100110100110110011001101011100110101010101110011010111001101101011 1 1 0 0
1101011100110101010101110011010111001101101010111001101011001101010101110 0 1 1 0 1 0 1 0
1110011010111001101010101011100110101110011011010111001101011111100110100 1 0 1 1 0 0
1010011011001100110101110010100110110111001101010101110011010111001101101 0 1
1111001101011100110100101001011011001110011010101010101011100110111001010 1 1 0 0 1 0 1
1100110011010010110110010100111110011010101010111001101011010010110010010 0 1 1 0
1100111001101001110011100110101010101010111001101011001010111001101010111 1 0 0 1 1
0111000001111101110011011010110110010101010101110011010101110111001101010 1 0 1 1 0 0 1
1010111001101101010010101010101100110101111100111110011011100101011100110 0 1 1 0 1 0
0110110001010011110011010101010111001101011100110100101101100101001011001 1 0 0 1 1 0
1010101010111001101110010101110011001101001011011001010011011001110011010 1 1 0 0 1
1010101011100110101110011011010111110011010111001101010101110011010111001 1 0 1 1
0101110011010110011010101010111001101011100110100110110010100110111001101 0 1 1 1 1 1
0000001101110011100110101010101010111001101110010101110011101010101011001 0 1 0 1 0
1010111001101110010101110011001101001010111001101001101100101001011100110 1 0 1
1111000000110111001110011010101010100110101010101011100110111001010111001 1 1 0 1 0 1
0101011100101010101011100110111001010101011100110111001010111001101010101 0 1 1
1001010101010111001101111001010111001100110100110110010100110110111001011 0 0 1 1
0011010011011001010011110011010101011001101011010111001101010101011001101 0 1 1
1001101101011100110101111111001101011100110101010111001101011001101101011 1 0 1 1
1001101010101011100110101110011011010111100110101110011010010101001010111 0 0 1 1 0
1001101100110011010111001101010100101010101010111001101110010101110011010 1
0101011100101010101011100110111001010111001101011001101101010111100110101 1 1
0011010101011100110101110011011010111001101010010110101010111001101010111 0 0 1 1 0
1011100110101010111001101011100110110101110011010111110011010011011001010 0 1 1 0 1
1001110011010111001101001101101110011010101011100110101110011011010111110 0 1 1 0 1

Graph

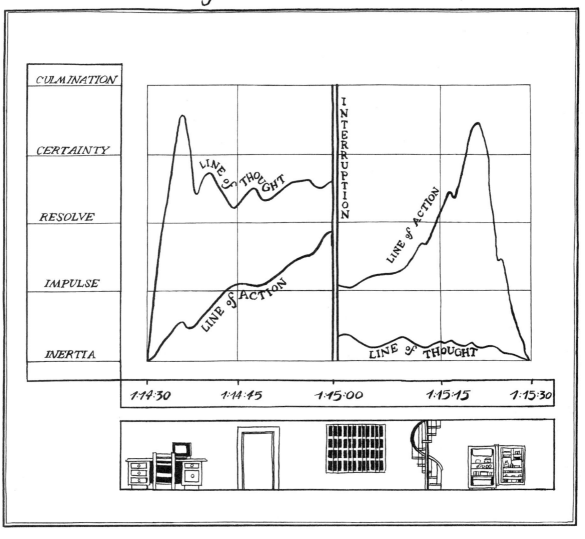

CHART Representing the EFFECT of an INTERRUPTION on a THOUGHT/ACTION Process as It Moves Through SPACE and TIME

In Case of Exercises in Style

Storyboard

Shot # 1

DOLLY BACK slightly as MATT rises and
closes LAPTOP.

Shot # 2

MED. SHOT of MATT coming through
DOORWAY. PAN LEFT as he moves into
DINING ROOM.

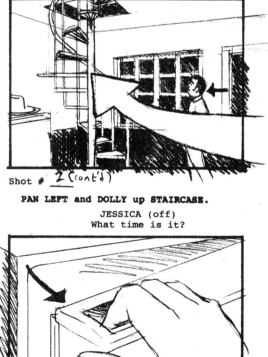

Shot # 2 (cont'd)

PAN LEFT and DOLLY up STAIRCASE.

JESSICA (off)
What time is it?

Shot # 3

CLOSE UP of MATT looking at WATCH.

MATT
It's 1:15.

Shot # 4

**EXTREME CLOSE UP of MATT'S HAND opening
REFRIGERATOR DOOR.**

JESSICA (off)
Thanks!

Shot # 5

Slow ZOOM/DOLLY into MATT as he
realizes he can't remember what the
hell he was looking for anyway.
FADE TO BLACK.

Brought to You by . . .

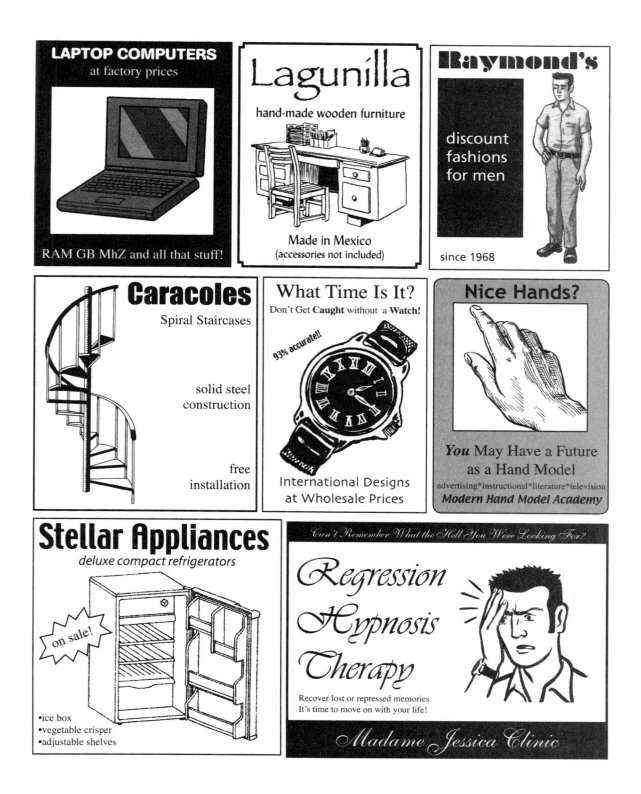

Calligram

in
mid-click a synapse
fires somewhere causing me to
abruptly put my work to sleep. You
interrupt me en   route wanting to
know how   long you have
been   procrastinating. I
oblige happily
after a quick
comparison
of big and
small.
However,
when I open
and peer
inside the
refrigerator
door I find I
can no longer
remember
what the
hell I was
looking
for,

any-
way.

No Pictures
(after Kenneth Koch)

Personification

The Next Day

Nested Stories

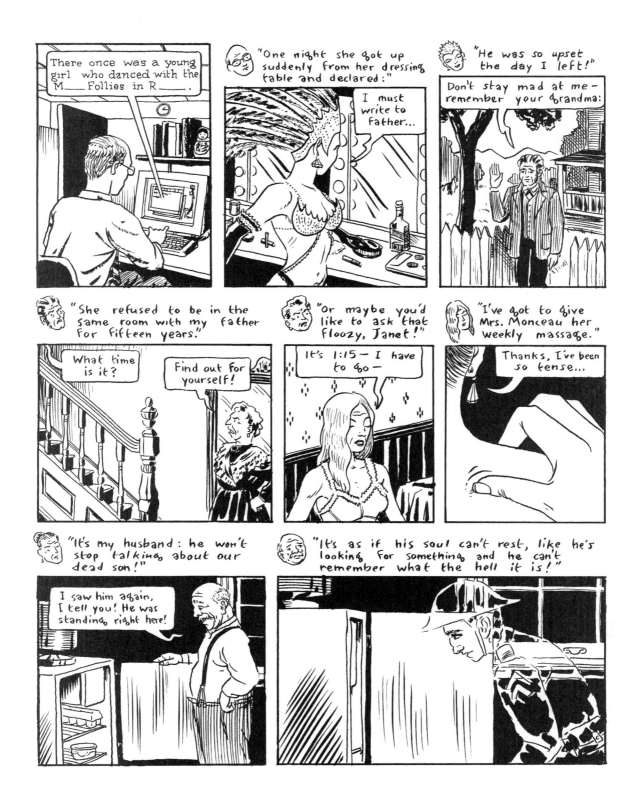

Overheard in a Bar

Happy Couple

Unhappy Couple

A Life

Around the World

The Critic

Evolution

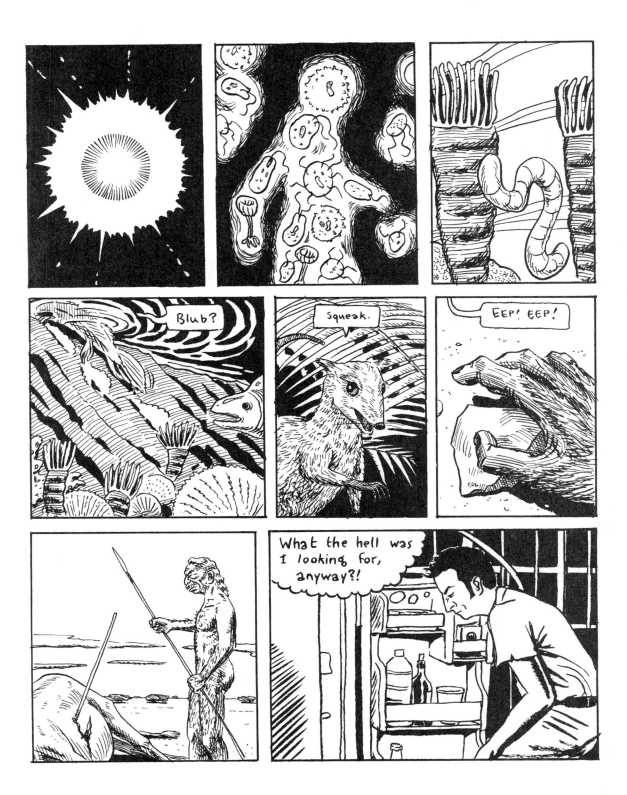

Creationism

A Lifetime to Get to the Refrigerator

Actor's Studio I

Actor's Studio II

Horizontal

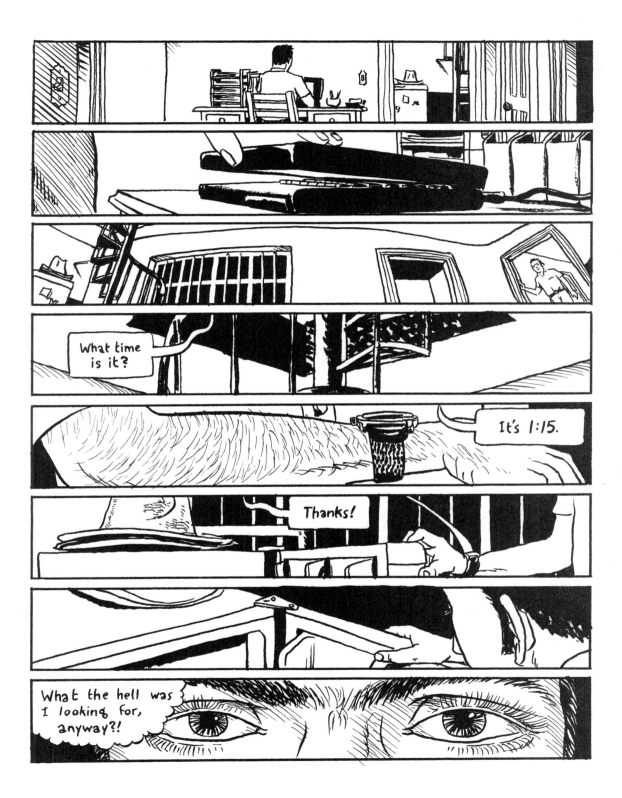

Vertical

Extreme Close-Ups

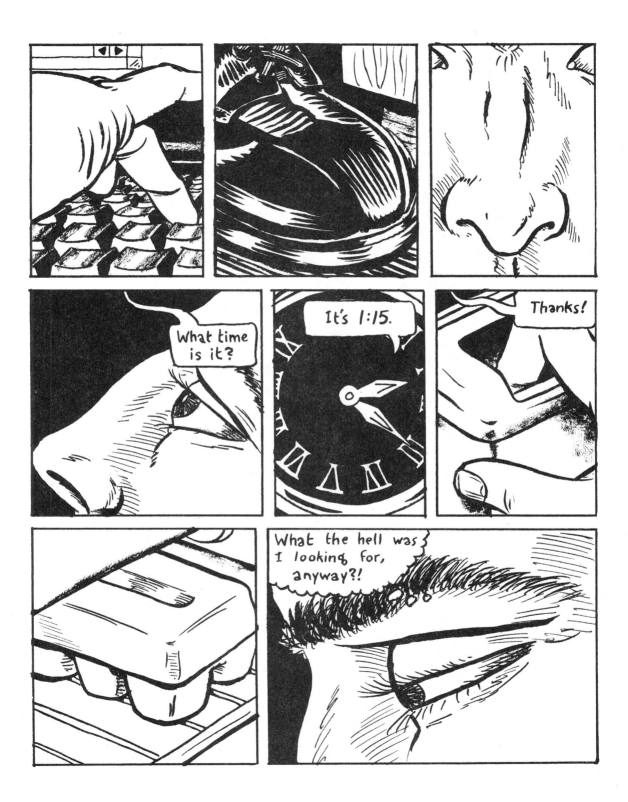

Long Shots

Extreme Zoom

Things Are Queer
(after Duane Michals)

Isometric Projection

Our House

One Horizon

Too Much Text

No Line

Silhouette

Minimalist

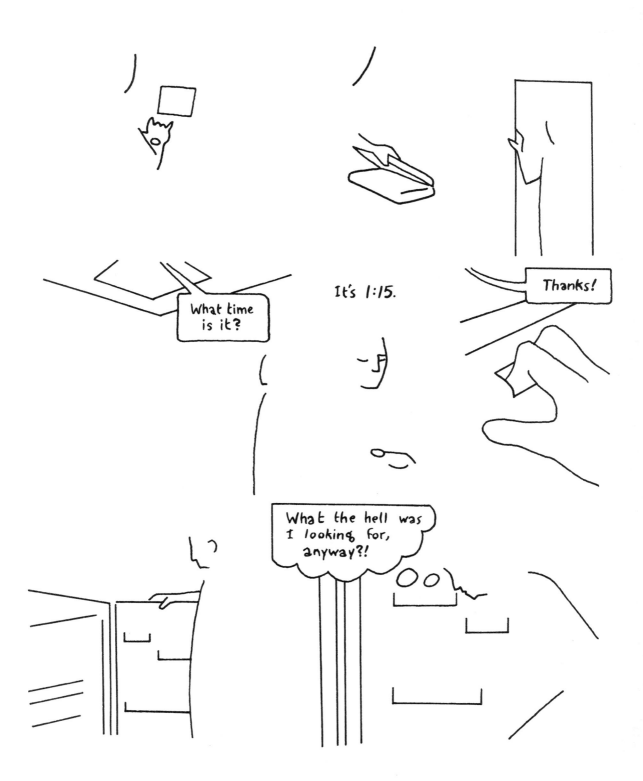

Maximalist

Fixed Point in Space

Fixed Point in Time

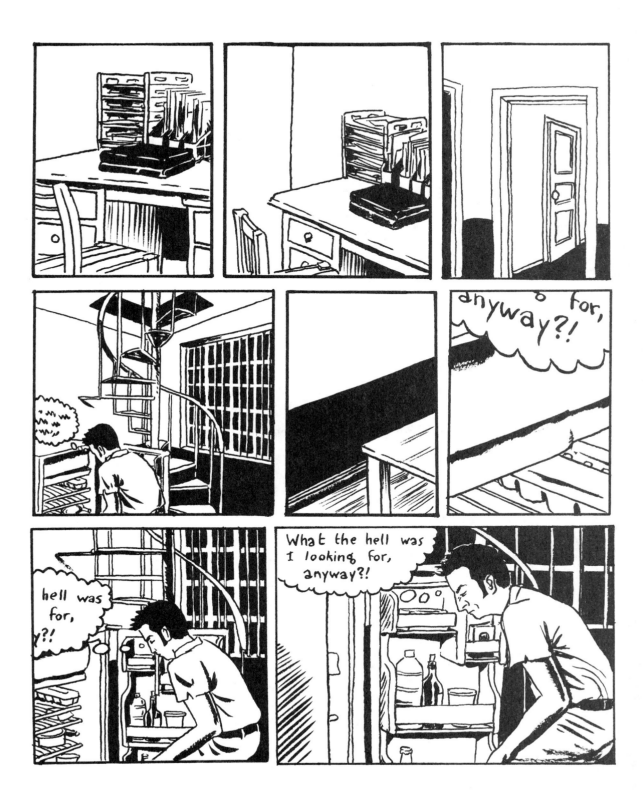

What's Wrong with This Comic?
(Two Changes in Every Panel)

Different Text

Different Images

No Refrigerator

No Jessica

No Matt

Notes on Some
of the Exercises

Emanata (p. 17):

This neologism is used by many cartoonists to describe the motion lines, flying sweat beads, and stars that are so characteristic of comics. The word was coined by cartoonist Mort Walker (b. 1923) in his *Lexicon of Comicana*, a tongue-in-cheek taxonomy which gives individual names to all sorts of marks and squiggles that have specific meaning in comics. "emanata" is actually intended as just one of these words—denoting squiggly lines that emanate from the head and end with musical notes (for whistling), hearts (for people in love) and so on—but it has been adopted by many cartoonists as the generic term, instead of Walker's own "comicana."

Photocomic (p. 39):

The photocomic (also referred to as a *fumetto* or *fotonovela*) has never had a large presence in the United States, but in Europe and Latin America it has a long history as a source of pulpy, murkily printed soap operas and masked wrestler adventures.

Manga (p. 43):

Manga is Japanese for "comic." Note that, being a Japanese version, this comic reads from right to left! The translation and sound effects were done by my friend Tomofusa Sato. Here's how to read the sound effects: Panel 1: Kacha Kacha; Panel 2: Patan; Panel 3: Zap; Panel 6: Kata; Panel 8: Boooon.

Furry (p. 59):

Anthropomorphism has a long and rich history in comics, from Mickey to Maus. This comic has a little fun with the subgenre/subculture known as "furries." (Look in any internet search engine for more information than you could possibly care to have.)

Anagrams (p. 77, 79):

An anagram is a word or phrase whose letters are rearranged to form a new phrase or word. "Anagram I" rearranges the panels and the words within their corresponding balloons, while "Anagram II" rearranges every individual element of the comic: letters, panel borders, objects, and so on.

Rodolphe Töppfer (p. 81):

Rodolphe Töppfer (1799–1846) was a Swiss educator and cartoonist considered by many to be the founder of the modern comic, based on a series of satirical pamphlets he published in the 1830s including *Histoire de M. Jabot* (1833) and *Les Amours de M. Vieuxbois* (1839). The latter book was published in an unauthorized English edition (as were many of his books) known as *The Adventures of Mr. Obadiah Oldbuck*.

A Newly Discovered Fragment of the Bayeux Tapestry (p. 83):

The Bayeux Tapestry was made in the eleventh century to comemmorate the Battle of Hastings (1066). It is often cited as a precursor to comics because of its "strip" form, its linear narrative continuity, and its combination of text and image.

What Happens When the Ice Truck Comes to Hogan's Alley (p. 85):

"Hogan's Alley" was a newspaper cartoon created by Richard F. Outcault (1863–1928). It introduced one of the icons of the comics medium, the Yellow Kid, and was at the center of the infamous newspaper power struggles between William Randolph Hearst and Joseph Pulitzer at the turn of the twentieth century.

Exorcise in Style (p. 87):

This comic is a tribute to *Tales from the Crypt*, and more generally to the influential batch of lurid horror, science fiction, and other genre comics published by EC comics in the 1950s.

Dynamic Constraint (p. 89):

Surely one of the most famous print advertising campaigns of all time, comics promoting the Charles Atlas bodybuilding course were a common feature of comics and magazines throughout the latter half of the twentieth century.

Ligne Claire (p. 91):

Ligne claire or "clear line" is a term introduced by European comics critics in the 1970s to describe comics that emphasized a clean graphic style, clear storytelling, and flat colors. The originator of the style remains its best: the Belgian Georges Remi, aka Hergé (1907–1983), creator of *The Adventures of Tintin*.

Exercises of a Rarebit Fiend (p. 99):

Winsor McCay (1869–1934) was an early cartoonist and animator, and the creator of "Little Nemo in Slumberland", "Gertie the Dinosaur," and "Dreams of a Rarebit Fiend," which inspired this strip.

Esk Her Size end Style (p. 101):

George Herriman (1880–1944) was the creator of *Krazy Kat*, widely acknowledged as one of the all-time high-water marks in comics, even though it was hardly read in its time.

Homage to Jack Kirby (p. 103):

Jack "King" Kirby (1917–1994) is considered one of the all-time great comic book artists. He is perhaps best known as the co-creator of such superheroes as the Fantastic Four and Captain America.

Exercises in Closure (p. 105):

This comic is a tribute to Scott McCloud's epochal *Understanding Comics* (Perennial Currents) and its most important contribution to the discussion of comics: the concept of "closure," referring to the connection the mind makes between two panels, allowing the creation of narrative meaning.

Cento (p. 111):

A *cento* (pronounced "sento," from the Latin for "patchwork") is a poem made up entirely of lines quoted from another poet.

Two in One (p.113):

This comic fuses my story with the one Raymond Queneau used for the original prose *Exercises in Style* (available in English from New Directions).

Calligram (p.125):

A calligram is a poem where the body of the text is laid out in such a way as to create a silhouette-like image.

No Pictures (p.127):

This comic was inspired by the "comics mainly without pictures," of poet Kenneth Koch (1925–2002), which fuse the languages of poetry and comics in novel ways. They were collected in a book called *The Art of the Possible* (Soft Skull Press).

Around the World (p.143):

The specific path this comic follows moves due east along roughly the 15th parallel north of the equator. The places visited are: Cuba, Cape Verde, Mali, Saudi Arabia, India, China (Hong Kong), Hawaii, and Mexico.

Things Are Queer (p.167):

This comic, a kind of perpetual zoom loop, was inspired by a series of photographs (from which I also borrowed the title) by Duane Michals (b. 1932), who has created many comics-like, multi-photo narrative sequences in his work.

Isometric Projection (p.169):

In an isometric projection all three faces are equally inclined to the drawing surface and parallel lines do not converge on a horizontal line.

What's Wrong with This Comic? (p.189):

Panel 1: chair missing back slat; extra paper tray

Panel 2: no sideburn; no watch

Panel 3: no belt; watch on opposite hand

Panel 4: staircase flipped, magnets re-arranged

Panel 5: shirt pocket gone; no painted wainscoting

Panel 6: no ring finger; tail of word balloon moved

Panel 7: giant sombrero; no support bar on staircase

Panel 8: no wine bottle; no bannister

Different Text (p.191):

The text I substituted here is a paraphrase of a wonderful one page strip from the book *Jack Survives* by Jerry Moriarity (b. 1938) (Raw Books and Graphics).

Acknowledgments

Thanks:

Nicholas Breutzman, Desmond Brice, Chester Brown, Daniel Clowes,
Shanna Compton, Marina Corral, Julie Doucet, Max Fenton, Stephen Frug,
Giancarlo Goria, Thierry Groensteen, Gene Kannenberg, Jr., Ben Katchor,
Yasmeen Khan, David Lasky, Jason Little, Jeff Mason, Marc-Antoine Mathieu,
David Mazzucchelli, Scott McCloud, Tom Motley, Gary Panter, Thomas Ragon,
Tomofusa Sato, Art Spiegelman, Gregory Trowbridge, Chris Waldron

Special Thanks:

Dominick Abel, Jessica Abel, Sally and Don Madden,
Andrew and Peter Madden, Bob Mecoy, Charles Orr

About the Author

Matt Madden started self-publishing minicomics in the early 1990s. He produced his first graphic novel, *Black Candy* (Black Eye Books) in 1998, and in 2001 published *Odds Off* (Highwater Books). Madden lives in Brooklyn with his wife, the author and cartoonist Jessica Abel. He works in comics and illustration, and teaches at both the School of Visual Arts and Yale University. His latest works appear in *A Fine Mess*, his bi-annual series published by Alternative Comics. You can learn more about him at www.mattmadden.com or www.exercisesinstyle.com.